A duck and a drake had a nest by a lake.

One rainy day, a snake
came to the nest.

The duck got away but the snake got the drake.

"Let go of my tail," said the drake. "No," said the snake. "I am going to eat you."

"Will you eat me with some cake?" said the drake. "That is the best way to eat drake."

"I can't make cake," said the snake.

"But Raven can make cake," said the drake.

"Raven's cake is yummy," said the drake.

"He makes it every day."

"What is in Raven's cake?" said the snake.

"Grapes and dates and raisins," said the drake.

"Yum yum," said the snake. "What a shame I can't fly to Raven's nest."

"But I can fly," said the drake.
"If you wait, I can get you some of
Raven's yummy cake."

"Okay. I will wait," said the snake, and he let the drake get away.

Snake lay and waited. He waited all day. But the drake did not come back.

Snake is still waiting.